Under the Microscope

...ersey and Kate Tym

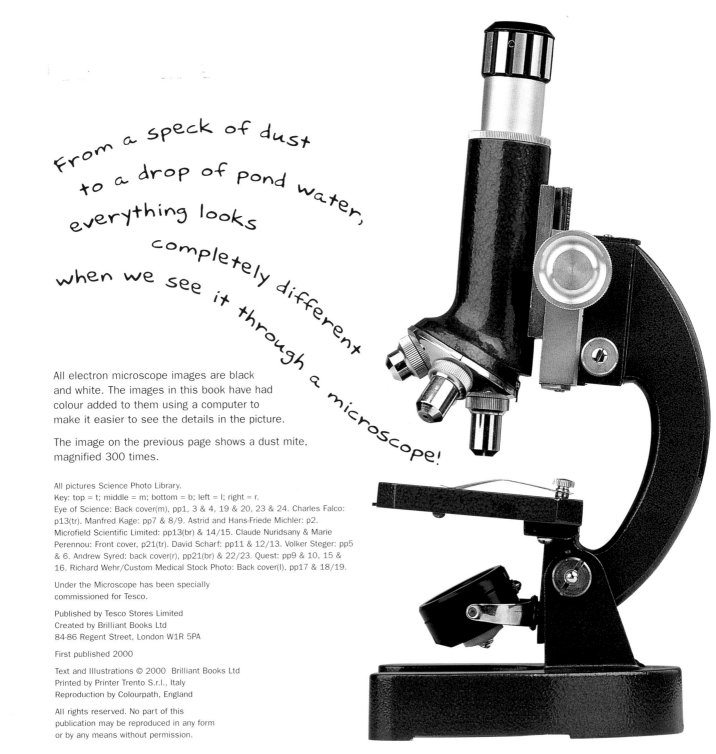

From a speck of dust to a drop of pond water, everything looks completely different when we see it through a microscope!

All electron microscope images are black and white. The images in this book have had colour added to them using a computer to make it easier to see the details in the picture.

The image on the previous page shows a dust mite, magnified 300 times.

All pictures Science Photo Library.
Key: top = t; middle = m; bottom = b; left = l; right = r.
Eye of Science: Back cover(m), pp1, 3 & 4, 19 & 20, 23 & 24. Charles Falco: p13(tr). Manfred Kage: pp7 & 8/9. Astrid and Hans-Friede Michler: p2. Microfield Scientific Limited: pp13(br) & 14/15. Claude Nuridsany & Marie Perennou: Front cover, p21(tr). David Scharf: pp11 & 12/13. Volker Steger: pp5 & 6. Andrew Syred: back cover(r), pp21(br) & 22/23. Quest: pp9 & 10, 15 & 16. Richard Wehr/Custom Medical Stock Photo: Back cover(l), pp17 & 18/19.

Under the Microscope has been specially commissioned for Tesco.

Published by Tesco Stores Limited
Created by Brilliant Books Ltd
84-86 Regent Street, London W1R 5PA

First published 2000

Text and Illustrations © 2000 Brilliant Books Ltd
Printed by Printer Trento S.r.l., Italy
Reproduction by Colourpath, England

Get in Focus

A microscope works like a very powerful magnifying glass, allowing us to see incredibly tiny things in amazing detail.

Until the microscope was invented in 1590, people used to think that fleas were made of dust and dirt! And for centuries, no one had any idea that many illnesses were caused by germs; if people couldn't see something, they naturally made the assumption there was nothing there to see.

The first microscopes were made just by putting two or three magnifying glasses together, but they were still powerful enough to let people see all sorts of tiny bugs and bacteria for the first time. Eventually, doctors were able to find ways to prevent or cure all sorts of terrible diseases. And detectives were able to compare a suspect's hair or blood sample with those left at a crime scene. A tuft of cloth caught on a fence can now make the difference between cracking a case or having to leave it unsolved.

The technology that surrounds us – such as mobile phones, cameras and personal organisers – just keeps on getting smaller and smaller. But we've only been able to develop all this miniature technology because of our ability to view microscopic things.

Without microscopes, we'd have no games consoles or computers and very few cures for diseases. Life would be harder for everyone – and a lot less fun, too!

Can you guess what this is?

Clue: Don't be a nitwit!

It's a louse

Lice live on the human body and also in people's hair.

Attractive aren't they?! And clever too... They lay their eggs (called nits) on your head. The eggs are tacky and stick to each other like glue, as well as to individual strands of hair. Once hatched, lice can multiply rapidly and – as anyone who's had nits or lice will know – the more there are, the more they itch! And unfortunately, they like clean hair just as much as dirty hair!

Each of the louse's legs ends in a strong claw – perfect for gripping a slippery hair when anyone tries to comb them out! But don't worry, even though lice are easily spread from one person to another, they're also pretty easy to get rid of. A good scrub with a special shampoo should have them running for cover in no time at all.

Lice feed about five times a day on a delicious meal of human blood.

Can you guess what this is?

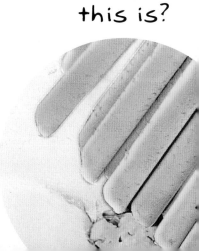

Clue: Smile!

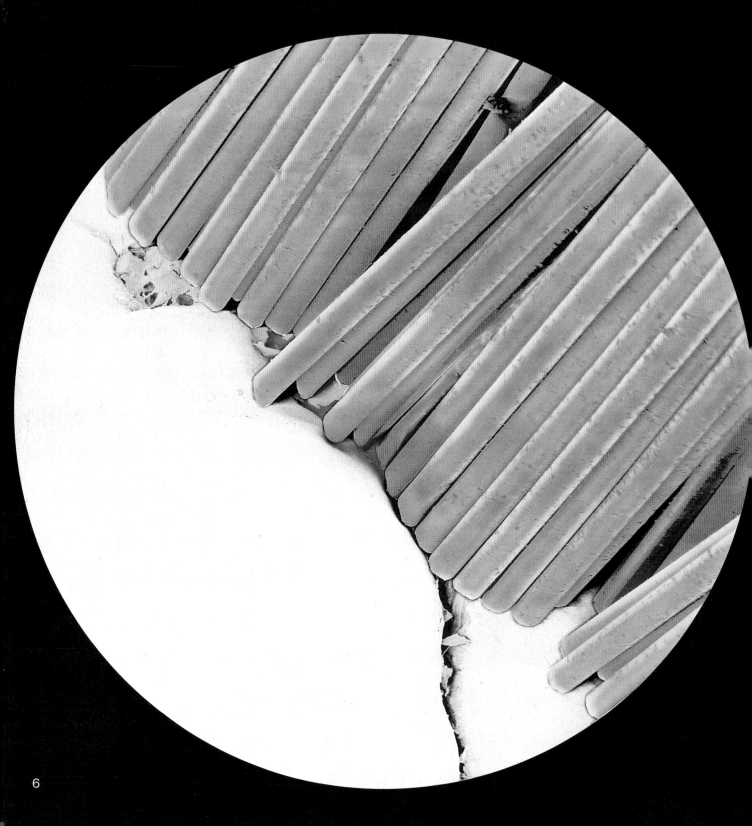

6

It's a tooth

Enamel, which covers the outside of all your teeth, is the hardest material in your body!

The picture shows a tooth being brushed. You can see the green food remains being brushed away by the bristles of the toothbrush. The tough outer layer of enamel protects the soft middle part of the tooth which contains nerves and blood vessels.

Bacteria are present everywhere – they're even in your mouth and on all food that comes into it. They love feeding on sugary things, and as they do, they make a coating on your teeth called plaque, which eats away at your enamel. So the more sweet things you eat, the more of your enamel they'll have for dinner! And once they've eaten through your enamel they'll get on your nerves – literally – and that means toothache!

Some dental drills are diamond-tipped to make them strong enough to drill through your enamel.

Can you guess what this is?

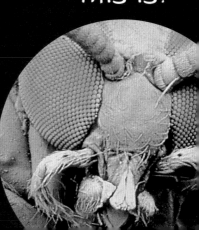

Clue: Buzz off!

It's a fly

Flies are amazing! They can suck up food and walk across your ceiling, and their wings beat at an incredible 200 times per second!

A fly's head is dominated by its massive eyes. Each one has about 4,000 separate lenses (ours just have one!). Placed on the side of the fly's head, they provide excellent all-round vision – which is one reason why they're so difficult to swat!

Flies are very dirty and carry a lot of nasty germs. In fact, the common house-fly is capable of carrying 30 well-known diseases (from leprosy to bubonic plague) and can even pass on parasitic worms to humans. Which is not surprising, as they're quite happy to go from sniffing something you'd rather not tread in, to walking right across your dinner!

The hairs on a fly's legs act as sensors which warn the fly if there is a sudden movement!

An adult fly will usually try to lay its eggs on a handy source of food. Then, when they hatch into squirmy maggots, they can start feeding straight away. Which is why it's best to keep foods covered up – especially in summer.

Flies suck up their food through their tube-like mouthpart. If they find liquid food, they're in luck, but if they find solid food, they have to dissolve it first with special juices, before they're able to get stuck in and start slurping!

Flies can walk on the ceiling because they have two sharp claws on each foot, which they can use to grip on to almost any surface. Their feet are also equipped with suction pads, which help them stick to smooth surfaces like glass or plastic.

Can you guess what this is?

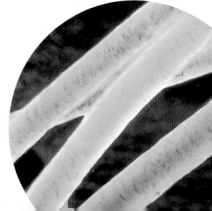

Clue: Blink and you'll miss it!

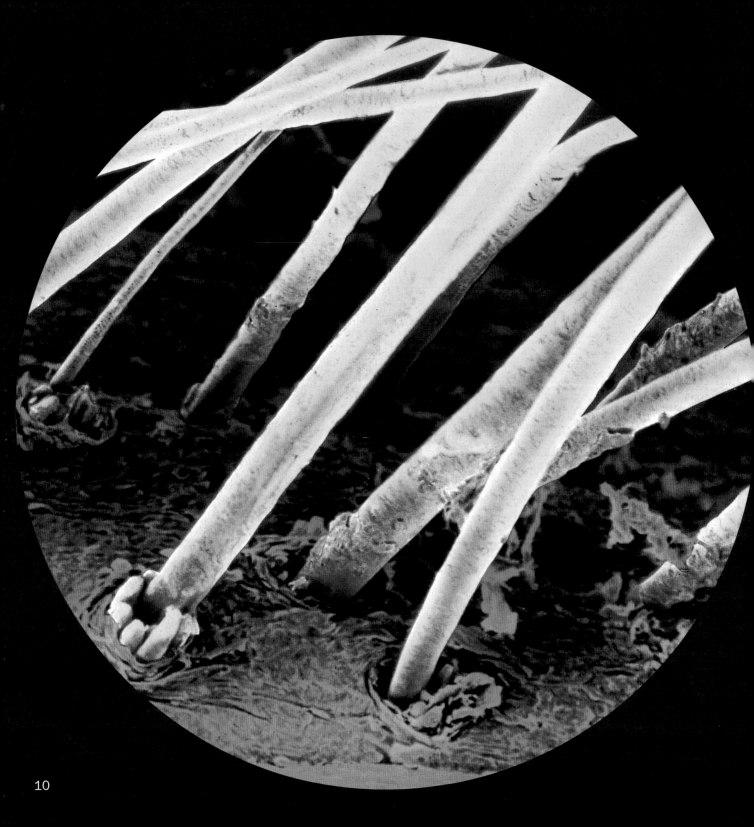

10

They're eyelashes

Eyelashes help to stop things from getting into your eyes – like dirt, dust and jumper fluff.

The eyelashes start to grow at a point below the skin called the follicle. The loose, straggly bits you can see are tiny flakes of dead skin, which break off as the hair pushes up through the hole in the skin which it grows out of. The hair that makes up your eyelashes and eyebrows, as well as the hair that grows in your nose, is called terminal hair – this is coarser than the hair on your head and the downy hair on the rest of your body. These coarser hairs protect your sensitive eyes and nose from irritation, as well as from bacteria and germs. If something is in danger of getting into your eyes, your eyelids blink automatically – and at the same time they also provide a nice, soothing wash.

your whole body is covered in hairs – only the palms of your hands and the soles of your feet don't have any!

Can you guess what this is?

Clue: Fish and...

It's a
microchip

Microchips are the nerve-centres for all kinds of electronic devices.

Microchips are made from tiny wafers of something called silicon. This close-up is of a microchip – magnified 1,300 times – and shows just a little bit of one of the many circuits on a 'chip'. Every circuit is like a network of microscopic roads, along which electronic messages zoom around.

Although computers are not really that clever, microchips help to make them very fast. A computer solves every problem by just saying yes or no; every time it says 'yes', a microscopic 'switch' in a circuit is turned on, and every time it says 'no', a switch is turned off. One chip contains hundreds of thousands of these switches and by turning them on and off in different combinations, a microchip can perform all kinds of tasks; from running the most powerful computers in the world, to making your toast pop up before it gets burnt!

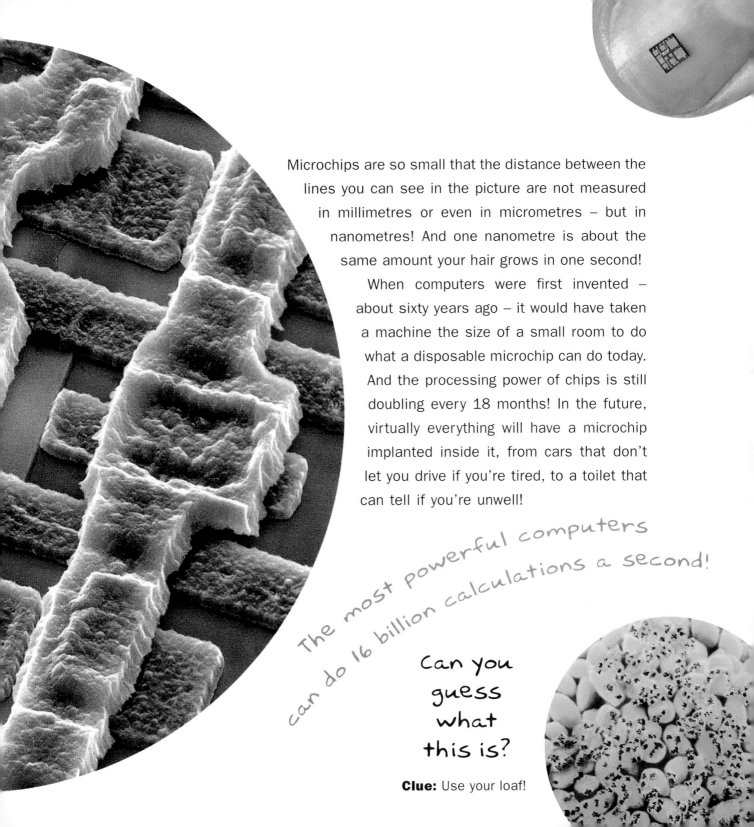

Microchips are so small that the distance between the lines you can see in the picture are not measured in millimetres or even in micrometres – but in nanometres! And one nanometre is about the same amount your hair grows in one second!

When computers were first invented – about sixty years ago – it would have taken a machine the size of a small room to do what a disposable microchip can do today. And the processing power of chips is still doubling every 18 months! In the future, virtually everything will have a microchip implanted inside it, from cars that don't let you drive if you're tired, to a toilet that can tell if you're unwell!

The most powerful computers can do 16 billion calculations a second!

Can you guess what this is?

Clue: Use your loaf!

It's mould

Mould can be nasty – like the stuff you find on a rotten orange in the fruit bowl. But it can be good too...

Mould is a type of fungus – like mushrooms and toadstools. It can spring up anywhere – from a damp mildew-covered wall to a tree with Dutch elm disease. It is made up of the colourful bits above the ground that we can see (called fruiting bodies), and a tangle of threads which spread out below the surface. Although a lot of moulds are harmful to us, some can actually do us good! Penicillin is an example of a 'friendly' mould – it's used to make antibiotics which can kill all sorts of nasty bacteria.

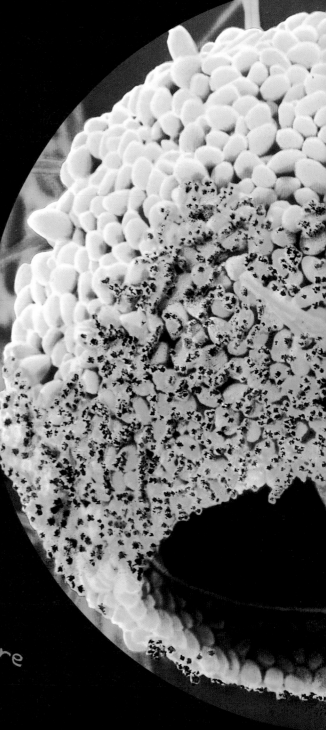

Humans can go mouldy – athlete's foot and ringworm are actually fungal infections!

The blue veins in cheeses like Stilton are... mould!

This picture shows the fruiting body of bread mould. It's been feeding and growing on an old slice of bread and now it's ready to spread elsewhere, by sending its spores out into the air. If the tiny spores land on something suitable for them to feed on, they'll grow in number and join up by forming a stringy web. As the mould feeds, it sends out chemicals which make the food it's living on begin to rot, which is why eating mouldy food is usually a very bad idea.

Mould serves as a visual warning that food is no longer good to eat. But if you think you can just cut out the mouldy bit – think again! The roots of the mould may still be there when you take a bite – yuck!

Can you guess what this is?

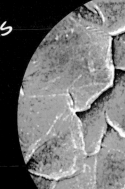

Clue: It's on the tip of my...

It's a
taste bud

There are more than 10,000 taste buds on the human tongue, each containing 50-75 taste cells.

The taste cells on the front of the tongue are more sensitive to sweet and salty flavours, while those up the sides detect sour and bitter ones. The most sensitive cells are found mainly at the back of the tongue, but no taste bud can pick up the flavours of food unless it has been dissolved in saliva.

Our sense of smell and touch, as well as the temperature of what we're eating, also help to add to our ability to taste. That's why you can't really taste anything properly when you've got a very bunged up nose. And a cup of cold soup will taste quite different from when it was piping hot!

It's really our sense of smell that we rely on to pick up most flavours. Try blindfolding your friend and holding a raw onion under their nose while feeding them some grated carrot – they will probably think they're tasting onion!

Taste bud cells only last a week before they are renewed.

Can you guess what this is?

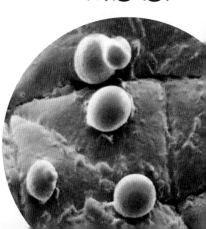

Clue: Your birthday suit!

It's human skin

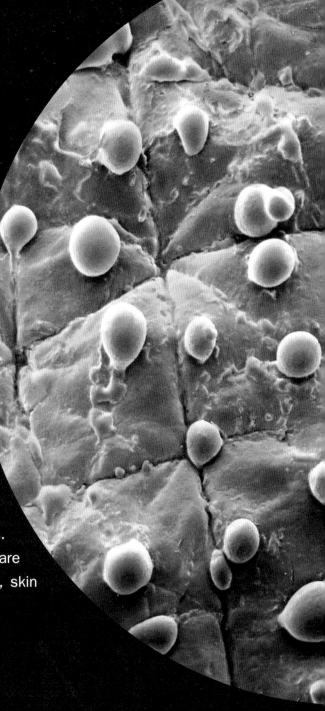

The skin is the largest organ of the body – weighing in at around two and a half kilograms! It's designed to keep our insides in and just about everything else out!

The skin does a brilliant job as the body's protective barrier. It acts as a waterproof covering for the rest of the body and also makes it more difficult for dirt and nasty germs and bacteria to get inside it. On top of that, skin protects people from the sun's ultra-violet rays. And by producing little beads of sweat, which are released through holes in the skin called pores, skin also helps to stop people getting too hot.

Did you know...
that every day we shed
about 50g of skin cells?

The picture on the left shows little droplets of sweat on the skin's surface, which help to cool the body down as they evaporate.

Sweat doesn't smell when it comes out of your pores. It's only after it's been lying around on your skin or on your clothes for a while and gets broken down by bacteria that it will probably start to pong a bit!

Skin is made up of several layers of skin cells which are constantly moving up to the surface, then dying and dropping off. The life-cycle of your skin – renewing and shedding, renewing and shedding – takes between 21 and 28 days. But in young people the process is quicker, which is why babies have such lovely soft skin!

Can you guess
what this is?

Clue: Beautiful flier.

It's a
butterfly

Butterflies' wings may look smooth, but in fact they are made up of thousands of tiny 'scales'.

Every scale on a butterfly's wing has its own unique colouring and shimmers as it reflects the light. Butterfly wings may seem to be delicate, but don't be fooled, they're surprisingly strong and Monarch butterflies make journeys of thousands of miles!

Some butterflies use their colouring as a form of camouflage – helping them hide from their enemies by blending into the background. Others have wings that look like a big, scary pair of eyes – designed to keep hungry predators away.

Every time a butterfly flaps its wings, some of the tiny scales fall off, and as it gets older and loses more and more of its scales, its dramatic colour will gradually fade.

Some butterflies are poisonous. They use their bright colouring to say KEEP AWAY!

Can you guess what this is?

Clue: You won't see me for...

It's house dust

Believe it or not, this is the kind of dust you find on top of your wardrobe, under your bed or behind your TV.

When you think of dust, you probably think of the bland, grey fluffy stuff that gathers on your living-room mantelpiece or behind bits of old furniture, before someone gets round to a bit of spring-cleaning.

But boring-looking dust is actually made up of thousands and thousands of amazing bits and pieces. Quite a lot of them are really odd shapes and surprisingly brightly coloured, but by the time they all get blended together, they just look grey.

As much as 90% of your household dust is made up of dead skin particles

Dust is made up of lots of different things – hair, natural and manmade fibres, pollen grains, spiky insect scales and tiny bits of dirt. It can even contain some particles that have come all the way from outer space! But, amazingly, most of your household dust tends to be made up of flakes of dead skin that simply drop off you and your family throughout the day. Dust can bring on asthma attacks and other allergic reactions in some people. And wherever there is dust, there are dust mites (see the picture on page 1). These microscopic insects just love the flavour of dead human skin – so your household dust is like a feast to them. Yum yum yum!

Can you guess what this is?

Clue: Sweet dreams!

They're
bedbugs

These ugly little monsters, pictured on a normal sheet, just love sucking your blood while you're asleep! The only clue that they've been having a midnight feast, is if you feel a little bit itchy in the morning. Bedbugs can be found on even the cleanest mattresses and pillows, so perhaps this is one time when you'd be better off NOT looking through a microscope at all!